E300

P9-CFQ-185

Most High, Omnipotent, Good Lord.
Yours be the praise,
the glory, the honor, and all benediction.

All praise be yours, my Lord,

For Brothers Wind and Air
fair and stormy . . .

For Brother Fire,
who brightens up the night,
full of power and strength . . .

For Sister Earth Our Mother,
who feeds us in her sovereignty . . .

For our Sister Bodily Death,
from whom no man living can escape.

Canticle of the Sun
Francis of Assisi (1182-1226)

Sister DEATH

O'Kelley Whitaker

MOREHOUSE-BARLOW CO.

New York

© 1974 by Morehouse-Barlow Co.
14 East 41st St., New York, N.Y. 10017

ISBN 0-8192-1182-6

Library of Congress Catalog Card No.: 74-80381

Printed in the United States of America

To Betty

Together we have shared death and life!

PREFACE

An old Arizona gold prospector who disappeared in 1949 left a hand-written will awarding nearly a quarter of a million dollars to any individual or organization that produced "research or some other scientific proof of a soul of a human body which leaves at death." To date, the money has not been awarded, although many persons and groups have tried to claim it.

Most of us share the old man's yearning for proof positive of life's continuing beyond death. This book lays no claim to the prospector's legacy. It offers no scientific proofs of life after death. Rather, it is written by one who has begun the exciting and often surprising adventure of faith in Jesus Christ. It is written for all who, however tentatively, have made a response to the living Lord and have entered into a relationship of faith with him. Its purpose is to begin to deal on the basis of the Christian Gospel with the re-

7

ality of our own death, as well as the deaths of those we love; to come to see the possibility of death in Christ as a *positive* rather than a destructive event; and to do so in terms that have meaning for us today.

The ultimate goal of this book, however, is not to try to satisfy curiosity about the unknowable but rather to assist in clarifying our beliefs about death in the light of Jesus Christ. Even one who considers life beyond death as true, or possible, or justifiable, without at the same time accepting the consequences of such commitment now, without progressing toward that new life which changes himself and the world—such a person has in fact denied for himself the power of that life. The quality of our living now is profoundly affected by what we really believe about the impact death has upon our own destiny.

This attempt to take a new look at the death of Christ and at our death in him grows out of the privileged intimacy a priest has with the living, the dying, and the bereaved, which for me during the past two decades has centered in four parishes of the Episcopal Church: St. Andrew's, Charlotte, North Carolina; St. Luke's, Salisbury, North Carolina; Emmanuel, Orlando, Florida; and now the Cathedral Church of St. Luke, Orlando. I am indebted to the Seabury Fellows program of Seabury–Western Theological Seminary, Evanston, Illinois, for the opportunity and resources of the seminary library for the original research, to my family for their support, and to many friends for their encouragement.

My prayer is that it will prove helpful to you as you continue to grow in fellowship with our Lord Jesus Christ and in the joy of the eternal life that is yours now in him.

O'Kelley Whitaker

Orlando, Florida
    Easter, 1974

Table of Contents

7   *Preface*

CHAPTER 1

13   *The Ultimate Question*

CHAPTER 2

20   *The Different Faces of Death*

CHAPTER 3

31   *The Good News of Jesus Christ*

CHAPTER 4

40   *The Good News of Jesus Christ, The First Problem*

CHAPTER 5

49   *The Good News of Jesus Christ, The Second Problem*

CHAPTER 6

57   *Eucharistic Living/Dying, The Offering, part A*

CHAPTER 7

67   *Eucharistic Living/Dying, The Offering, part B*

CHAPTER 8

76   *Eucharistic Living/Dying, The Consecration, part A*

CHAPTER 9

85   *Eucharistic Living/Dying, The Consecration, part B*

CHAPTER 10

92   *Eucharistic Living/Dying, The Communion*

CHAPTER 11

99   *Eucharistic Living/Dying, The Thanksgiving*

105   *Selected Bibliography*

109   *Funeral and Memorial Societies*

110   *Donor Card*

1

THE ULTIMATE QUESTION

"Was it for this the clay grew tall?"

Wilfred Owen (1893-1918)

It was mid-December. The bustle of Christmas preparations was everywhere. The telephone rang. An unfamiliar voice obviously more accustomed to giving crisp, military commands than to making requests introduced himself.

"This is Captain ——— of the United States Marine Corps. I am at the home of one of your parishioners. Can you come at once?"

"Is it about . . . ?"

"It is official business," he interrupted.

No more really needed to be said. The message came through loud and clear. The news reports were consumed with the bitter fighting in the Da Nang area. Suddenly Vietnam was here—not somewhere on the other side of the world. It was death that brought it close.

He was a bright-eyed, smiling young man when he left in the spring. The only child of his family, he had joined the Marine Corps because he had long wanted to be a Marine, and also, perhaps, because somehow things had not yet clicked for him in life. He needed time to mature. He needed to live and to grow and to discover himself. Now he was dead—dead before he had fully lived.

What is there to say about the death of the young? Life seems incomplete for them. But there it is. You cannot argue with it. In an earlier war, a young English officer in France shortly before his own death just before the Armistice expressed his grief for a fallen comrade in a poem he entitled "Futility."

> Move him into the sun—
> Gently its touch awoke him once,
> At home, whispering of fields unsown.
> Always it woke him, even in France,
> Until this morning and this snow.
> If anything might rouse him now
> The kind old sun will know.
>
> Think how it wakes the seeds—
> Woke, once, the clays of a cold star.
> Are limbs, so dear-achieved, are sides,
> Full-nerved—still warm—too hard to stir?
> Was it for this the clay grew tall?
> —O what made fatuous sunbeams toil
> To break earth's sleep at all?[1]

"Was it for this the clay grew tall?" Is this not our question whenever death comes "out of

---

[1] Wilfred Owen, *Collected Poems.* Copyright Chatto & Windus, Ltd., 1946, © 1963. Reprinted by permission of New Directions Publishing Corporation, New York.

season"? The bicycle on the highway edges into the line of traffic at just the wrong time. Leukemia attacks. An accident happens at play. An assassin tries to shape history—and succeeds. When death comes to the young, it seems as pointless, as useless, as destructive as picking a garden flower before the bud has begun to show its color. The flower is only in what might have been.

Yet the specter of death does not really change its form when it confronts older people. You can feel as well as hear the futility of life confronted by death. "You know what they say: 'It takes nine months to create a man, and only a single day to destroy him.' . . . Listen . . . it does not take nine months to make a man, it takes fifty years—fifty years of sacrifice, of determination, of—so many things! And when that man has been achieved, when there is no childishness left in him, nor any adolescence, when he is truly, utterly, a man—the only thing he is good for is to die."[2]

The older person can look at his life and consider what it might have been—the untapped potentialities, still there, but neither time nor strength left to explore them. Throughout life he has been making choices, and in his acts of choosing one way, he has forever abandoned other ways that might have been. The fullness of

[2]André Malraux, *Man's Estate*, quoted in Ladislaus Boros, S.J., *The Mystery of Death*. New York: The Seabury Press, 1965, p. vii.

life has somehow escaped him. All he can do is
hold on to what he has, deny any change, prevent
any further growth, holding tight until death
loosens his grasp of life forever. As age advances,
the process of death is recognized in the decline
of physical and mental abilities. Indeed, in a
greatly debilitated condition, death itself may be
welcomed, though the long act of dying still
leaves the big question: "What does it all add up
to?"

Death is the ultimate enemy—Paul said it,
and he is right. Whether we see death in the
young or in the old, or coming upon ourselves, it
forces us sooner or later to ask whether God
really runs this world or particularly cares about
human affairs. The popular interest some years
ago in "Death of God" theology lay not so much
in real appreciation of the often obscure thought
of those radical theologians as in a fascination
with associating the reality of death and our
basic doubts about God. We heard the catch
phrase "Death of God" used by professional re-
ligionists and responded inwardly, "O dear, it is
just as we had suspected and feared. God is not
there after all to make everything work out all
right in the end."

It is an ageless concern. Shakespeare puts the
profound question about death in the mouth of
Hamlet who, upon returning to Denmark from
exile, chances upon the gravedigger as he throws
up the skull of Yorick, the court jester of

Hamlet's boyhood. Suddenly Hamlet feels the shock of human mortality. Does this crumbling skull have anything to do with the man he had known and loved? Hamlet's thoughts move from Yorick to the great men of the past. Can Caesar, who once ruled the world, now be nothing more than a lump of common clay which someone may use to patch his house wall? Does all the glory and tragedy of history lead up to one last death rattle? Does the whole human enterprise add up to nothing? "Was it for this the clay grew tall?"

We live in an age that is both frightened and fascinated by death. Jean Paul Sartre, the French atheistic existentialist, contends that death is absurd, an irrational something that renders life itself irrational. Therefore, he says, we ought not to think about it. But most of us cannot ignore it. Sooner or later the threat of death confronts us with irresistible force. One contributing factor in our difficulty in facing death squarely is the climate in which we live. An articulate nurse, who has often been with the dying, comments, "A materialistic outlook finds it hard to contemplate death except perhaps in a sensational or sentimental way. A society occupied with the pursuit of prosperity, security and tangible pleasures has no valid answer to the problems of suffering and death and so the questions must not be asked."[3]

[3]Cicely Saunders, "And From Sudden Death...", *Frontier,* Vol. IV, Winter 1961, p. 271.

Another voice adds that the devil can use death either to crush men with a sense of frustration or to terrify them with a sense of inexorability. "It is because of these twisted and distorted views of death that men are afraid of death. The cruel annihilation of their ambitions, the rude termination of their material comfort and ease, the final separation from the objects of their desires—these are the aspects under which death is seen and through which it gains its terrors."[4]

In the face of an inner climate of doubt and an outer climate of anxiety, we Christians strangely *celebrate* a death, a death upon a cross, the execution of Jesus of Nazareth. As we celebrate his death, we are not particularly somber. We do not react with shock, for instance, as we did on November 22, 1963, when the assassination of a President was announced. When we gather as Christians in our churches we do not dress or conduct ourselves as at a funeral. Indeed, we proudly display the instrument of execution in many different ways. We do not mourn, but rather we rejoice. Even the day of Jesus' death we call *Good* Friday, not "Bad" or "Black" or "Gloomy" or "Mournful." Why, really, do we follow Christian tradition and impulse to call it "Good"? What is good about death? Do we look upon the Easter Resurrection as God's mighty ink remover that cancels out the ugly blot of the

[4]F. W. Dillistone, *Jesus and His Cross*. Philadelphia: Westminster Press, 1953, p. 32.

events of the Passion, the agony, the dying upon the cross? Do we say, "Well, the cross was very bad, it is true—but Easter made it good"? The truth is that we find the event on Golgotha very uncomfortable indeed; we do have trouble relating the bloody Good Friday cross upon which a man actually died to the clean, empty cross of Easter. There is a strong impulse to bypass Good Friday in favor of Easter.

When we gaze upon the cross, you see, we behold in the death of Jesus every man's death —the death of the young, the old—our own death. It is a disturbing view. Yet the impulse of the long Christian heritage has been to celebrate the death of its Lord, to call the day good, to show forth the instrument of execution as the symbol of loyalty and fellowship with him. Has Jesus then transformed death from a catastrophe into a positive event? Is it possible to look upon death in some way as friend instead of enemy?

2

THE DIFFERENT FACES OF DEATH

"Change and decay in all around I see;
O thou who changest not, abide with me."

H. F. Lyte

"God has fallen off the gravy train" is the caustic observation of one recent observer of the church and national scene. The Christian Church through the ages has made much of man's mortality, he continues, but now the Church no longer has "going for it" man's anxiety about death. Society is no longer frightened, but embarrassed, by dying. Modern man is a devotee of scientific secular humanism, and he no longer responds to fairy tale promises by Christianity.

Modern man no longer hears with conviction the classic Christian answers to "What happens when I die?" This is as true of the person in the pew as of the nonbeliever. Yet modern man has not in any way mitigated his fear of death. If anything, death is *more* threatening than ever before, simply because the old answers are gone and there is nothing to replace them or to give a person support in constructing some substitute conviction about his own end. Indeed, if the increasing frequency of studies, seminars, and reports on death and dying is a fair indication, anxiety about death is still very real.

A healthy development during the past decade has been the increasing willingness to look at death and discuss it objectively. Jessica Mitford was one of the early pioneers in bringing about the attitude shift with her publication of *The American Way of Death*[1] in 1963. More recently, in its 1970 Easter article on religion, *Newsweek* devoted five pages to "How America Lives with Death."[2] In this article psychologist Robert Kastenbaum is quoted as saying, "There is almost no relationship between what people think they think about death and how they really feel when they face it." As evidence he points to an experiment conducted by Wayne State's Center for Psychological Studies on Dying, Death and Lethal Behavior, during which a group of housewives expressed varying attitudes toward death which ranged "from stoic acceptance to rigorous faith in personal immortality." When they were invited to visit with patients, however, they talked readily with those they considered "merely sick," but invariably inched away from those they thought were dying and could not look at them directly. Clearly the subject generated too much personal anxiety to handle.

[1]New York: Simon and Schuster, 1963.
[2]April 6, 1970, pp. 81ff. Article by Kenneth L. Woodward.

Bereaved persons demonstrate a variety of attitudes toward death, attitudes that often have little or no root in Christian heritage. Some take
great comfort in the mortician's craftsmanship
and remark, "How peaceful he looks." This is
what they want to believe, and they often appear
to use self-hypnosis in seeking reassurance.
Others are repulsed by the artificiality of the
cosmetics, by the coldness and rigidity of the
form. They take comfort in the fact that the body
is not really the person—the personality, the
soul, has been released.

After a long and serious illness, or even a
short one in which much damage has been done
to the body, the fact of death is eased by the conviction that had the patient revived, his life
would have been miserable indeed in such a de-
fective body. Better dead than a vegetable! A
blessed release—but to what? Is it possible that
the *what* to which the deceased has been released
is worse than being a vegetable? But, of course,
that question is not posed, at least not consciously, not openly.

As people face their own deaths, some seek
comfort in the fact that their good works will
survive and continue to influence others. I have
never heard anyone comment on the continuing
influence of *bad* deeds! Others look to their children to further their lives, though one wonders
whether any child-become-man today ever looks
upon himself as a continuation of the lives of his
forefathers.

Nor has the fear of death been overcome by the fact that modern technology is able frequently to thwart death or at least delay it for a while. Modern technology has brought many benefits to men—for which we give thanks. But it has also tended to broaden and obscure many of the destructive causes of death. While antibiotics, for example, have curbed a great number of formerly fatal infections, the prolonging of life has in and of itself brought forth an increase of the malignancies and chronic diseases that often come with age.

The success of modern medicine has brought about moral dilemmas that did not have to be dealt with even a decade ago. The costly cryogenic freezing of bodies in the expectation that science will some day find a cure for death is, for economic reasons alone, a purely hypothetical question for most of us. Far more pertinent is the concern with how long life-support machines should stay on and maintain a life that will never be able to maintain itself. Should every effort be made to keep alive an infant for whom there is no hope of developing any kind of life that will provide even a measure of joy to himself or his family? Should a person have the "right to die" when he is utterly weary of fighting a losing battle against disease? The measures used to keep former President Harry Truman alive for the last three weeks of his life were extraordinary and have led some members of the medical profession publicly to question treatment that tends to transform a person into an extension of machines when there is no real hope of revival or recovery.

Death demands and gets international attention as a factor in human rights. Is there "a point beyond which intensive methods to keep incurably ill or very elderly patients alive should no longer be applied"? U Thant, while still Secretary-General of the United Nations, quoted the remark of a Warsaw surgery professor, Witold Rudowski, that a surgeon's work turns into cruelty "if he goes on prolonging a life that can never again have purpose or meaning" and that this is especially true "if the patient with an incurable condition wants to die." What about the cost of the sophisticated treatment often required, if the patient's family cannot afford it or if the cost, whether in dollars or personnel, limits medical care for others? Since medical technicians cannot serve everyone, who should be first to receive their benefits? Who should receive transplanted organs while they are scarce? Who will protect the donor of a transplant organ from premature removal of the organ?

This latter concern has already provoked debate as to when death really takes place, which is also the question the physician providing artificial life support must face. Does the moment of death occur after no possibility of recovery exists, but before a donated organ can be too impaired for use? An international conference of medical specialists and theologians meeting in Madrid in the summer of 1969 were unable to reach any agreement about the clinical definition of death.

Americans in particular are highly sensitive to the kind of technology that brings awesome death through mass forms of destruction against which no individual can prevail. The nuclear bomb, germ warfare, defoliation and anti-vegetation chemicals, napalm—all of these are much more fearful than a single, identifiable, specific enemy. Yet the threat of death in any form generates deep anxiety.

One of the ways we try to cover up an ever-growing fear of death, Dr. Rollo May asserts in *Love and Will*[3], is by an obsession with sex in our cultural lives. He holds that all men have the fear of death; all men have always had this fear. But because of our inability to cope single-handedly anymore with the causes of death, we tend to repress our awareness of death. At the same time, sex has become a way of life —moving pictures, theater, books, magazines, advertising—all become daily more graphic. Dr. May contends that "an obsession drains off anxiety from some other area and prevents the person from having to confront something distasteful. What would we have to see if we could cut through our obsessions about sex? That we must die. The clamor of sex all about us drowns out the ever-waiting presence of death."[4]

[3]New York: W. W. Norton & Company, 1969.
[4]*Ibid.*, p. 106.

One of the happier developments in the current confusion is the willingness of some of the medical, social, and pastoral disciplines to break the awful silence about death and take a serious and honest look—a look through the eyes of the person who is dying. Dr. Elisabeth Kübler-Ross has pioneered a clinical study of the terminally ill patient and also of the attitudes of the family and the professional staff who attend him. As a psychiatrist she worked with a group of medical and theological students, nurses, and social workers at the University of Chicago's Billings Hospital to study volunteer patients who were terminally ill and to learn from them what they feel and need during the process of dying. Her report *On Death and Dying*[5] is essential reading for everyone, professional and layman alike, who wants to develop some objectivity in dealing with those facing death.

In the report Dr. Kübler-Ross describes five reactions of a patient to dying, which can occur successively or in any grouping.

The first response is *denial:* "No, not me." This provides a patient the time he needs to recollect himself and to begin to face the awesome reality.

When denial can no longer be maintained, it is replaced by *anger:* "Why me?" This is a difficult time for the family and staff as well as the patient because the anger is vented in every di-

[5]New York: The Macmillan Company, 1969.

rection, against everyone, and calls for abundant understanding.

Bargaining is the third stage and one that is often difficult to detect. It is an attempt by the patient to put off the inevitable by having "one last chance," then another, and another.

After the bargaining stage, the patient is usually overcome by deep *depression* as he faces the great losses of his life, those already experienced because of his illness and those he is about to suffer because of his approaching death. Just a quiet, loving presence may be the most comforting support for him at this time.

The final stage is *acceptance,* " 'the final rest before the long journey' as one patient phrased it."[6] The patient has found peace and acceptance and his world of interest has decreased markedly to perhaps one or two persons. He is quiet. He is ready.

Hope is of overriding importance throughout these stages of progression, Dr. Kübler-Ross points out, disappearing only at the final one. A "last-minute success in a research project," "a miracle," "a new lease on life," "some extra time I did not ask for." The physician can often be the instrument, not of false hope, but of assurance that all is being done that can be, that he as a professional man will not desert the patient.

She also points out that the Church was formerly able to provide an even deeper hope. In

[6]*Ibid.,* p. 100.

other generations people have been more ready to believe in God and in a life that went beyond the grave, giving purpose and fulfillment to the incompleted earthly life. "There was a reward in heaven, and if we had suffered much here on earth we would be rewarded after death depending on the courage and grace, patience and dignity with which we had carried our burden."[7]

Dr. Melvin J. Krant of Tufts University describes in "The Organized Care of the Dying Patient"[8] a new training program in counselling dying patients and their families. The medical profession usually views its goal as the development of health, and thus death is considered a failure of the health care system. Dr. Krant shows that medical personnel, with others, have a ministry to the dying as well. "Helping someone die well should be conceived as a positive part of health care. . . . The terminal . . . patient, who has sojourned through so many hands and facilities, must finally come to a place where he is totally at home and from which he will not be sent on or be thrown back into the community unsupported. . . . To the focus on tumors, so to speak, we are adding a focus on lives."[9] This concern extends to the family of the terminal patient. The goal is to enable all who are concerned, including the attending doctors and nurses, to face death with some measure of

[7]*Ibid.*, p. 13.
[8]In *Hospital Practice*, Vol. 7, No. 1, January 1972.
[9]*Ibid.*, pp. 101ff.

psychological comfort. The difficulty with the professional person as well as the layman is the fact that no matter what we *say* to a dying person we communicate through our attitude and manner what we really believe about death, our "gut feeling." It is seldom what comes from above the neck that supports another person, but that which comes from below, from the heart of a man.

Providing emotional stability to the dying and to their families and friends, helping them to learn how to be supportive, how to *listen,* is a goal to which happily more and more of the medical profession are directing their attention. Doctors and other scientists are learning new skills in helping people to accept and deal with the inevitable. Dr. Kübler-Ross has affirmed that an additional factor is greatly needed, namely the *hope* that there is something good beyond the gate of death.

Such a hope is beyond the reaches of science. It is the Church's task and opportunity to proclaim that hope so that people today can receive it and respond to it The "pie in the sky" variety of hope is simply no longer valid. Can we Christians no longer affirm the hope that the death event itself has within it the promise of being not the end but a focal point for the final investment of all that we are as persons? It is the urgent function of the Church today amid the great fear of death to sense the need and to speak in words and concepts that can be understood, accepted, and personally appropriated.

To look at death with anything except fear, the man of faith must look at the one death that did not shut the door upon life but rather opened the way to life, the death of Jesus Christ.

3

THE GOOD NEWS OF JESUS CHRIST

"...we preach Christ crucified, a stumbling block to Jews and folly to Gentiles, but to those who are called, both Jews and Greeks, Christ the power of God and the wisdom of God."

I Corinthians 1:23, 24

In America today graveyards are not seen near newer church buildings. By contrast, old church-yards nearly always contain the graves of the saints who have gone before. There may be practical, even legal reasons for this change; but there is also a significant underlying symbol. The Church today is sorely tempted to preach a "gospel" that promises happiness without pain, beauty without ugliness, life without death. This is what the culture about us constantly holds before us—pain and sweat can be eliminated by the right pills and the proper spray. Thus the Church is intimidated into feeling that its gospel of life-only-through-death is a bit second rate. Many Christians, it appears, are convinced that much of traditional Christianity is really impractical, unrealistic, and no longer necessary. How

many churchmen really believe in new life—or
any kind of life—beyond the here and now? Sur-
veys indicate that today a large portion of regular
churchgoers do not believe in a personal life
beyond the grave. Since church members often
reflect the convictions of their ministers, no
doubt clergy themselves need to deal honestly
with their own deepest feelings and anxieties
about death and their hope for everlasting life.

The symbol of Christian faith from the beginning has been the cross, the cross of Jesus
Christ. This was not a natural or easy symbol for
the first Christians to accept or live with. The
cross was, of course, the basest instrument of execution, reserved for the lowest criminals. At
first it was frankly an embarrassment to the followers of Jesus, a stumbling block as Paul called
it. But once the Christian community could
overcome its embarrassment at the means of
Jesus' death and see the event in all its nobility,
it was Christ crucified who became the center of
preaching and faith. The sign nailed above the
head of Jesus on the cross at the command of Pilate, "The King of the Jews," was intended by
that Roman official to be a slur upon the Jews
and a mockery of the early followers of Jesus.
Yet, once those first disciples had accepted the
Lordship of Jesus, seen him indeed to be the
Christ, God's Messiah, the truth of the accusation could not be denied. Indeed, he was "King
of the Jews" in a beautiful new sense, a king

who exercised exclusively the power of self-giving love. Soon thereafter he was seen to be the kingly lover of all men everywhere, not merely of the Jews. So instead of minimizing the crucifixion, Christians proclaimed it, and the accusation written above Jesus' head was presented as an unintentional witness to his lordship. The Good News of Jesus Christ, as ironic today as it was then, is that he is a *crucified conqueror,* the living vindication of the transforming power of divine love.

Yet the cross remains a problem for every generation of Christians, and succeeding generations tend to view it differently. We have often disguised the cross in preserving it as a symbol. We have made it small, gilded it, redesigned it, adorned it, beautified it—until we have concealed fairly well the fact that it was originally a rough instrument of death as surely as a gallows or an electric chair. In obscuring the nature of the cross we also obscure the basic biblical emphasis. Read your New Testament with a score card and you will find that the words "crucifixion" and "death" appear about as often as the word "life." The fact of the cross, the fact of death, cannot be diminished without distorting the Good News of Jesus Christ.

The event of Good Friday, the narrative of the Passion, consumes a goodly portion of each Gospel, more in fact than the event of that first Easter Day. The death of Jesus is a critical focus

of each Gospel account as well as of the early
preaching of the Apostles as recorded in Acts.
Many Christians through the centuries have died
for upholding the claim that the death of Jesus
has profound significance for all men. Again and
again the New Testament affirms that Christ
died and that he died for our sins. It was for the
evil of humanity that he died, for the very forces
that killed him! This is a fundamental claim of
the Gospel, which cannot be ignored. If a man
dies in your behalf, you simply cannot ignore the
fact. You may think his act foolish, unnecessary,
or you may be grateful beyond measure—but you
simply cannot ignore the man or his deed.

Early in the Church's life and until fairly recent times, the tendency more and more was to
emphasize the tragedy rather than the victory of
the cross. Christian art through the ages has de-
picted more paintings, mosaics, crucifixes, and
sculptures of the emaciated, suffering Christ than
of the glorious King of Life. Feeling the power
of the cross, staggered by the implications that
exceed man's comprehension of the Son of God
accepting such humiliation, devout people
through the ages have tried to understand God's
reconciling action on Calvary. "By the cross you
are saved." But why did it have to be in such a
manner? How was the "at-one-ment" between
God and man achieved on the cross? How could
the death of God's only Son bring about reconciliation between God and his people and break

down the barriers that separate men from God and from each other?

The predominating answer was stated in terms of the eternal scales of justice, out of balance because of man's sin. Aware of his unworthiness and his inability to make up the deficit of love his sins had created, man could only turn humbly to Jesus, the perfect man, to cover his indebtedness and thus make reconciliation possible. The pure and perfect self-offering of Jesus could alone satisfy man's eternal debt to God's justice. From such an approach to the cross sprang such popular hymns as,

> There was no other good enough
> To pay the price of sin,
> He only could unlock the gate
> Of heav'n, and let us in.[1]

The suffering of Christ was the price that had to be paid for human waywardness, and man, conscious of the cost, could only be further indebted to God.

Christians who have lived through the decade of the 1960's have given clear evidence —both by involvement in and resistance to the great social efforts of that period—that they know they crucify the Lord every time they affront their neighbor economically, socially, politically, or educationally. Many suffer a profound sense of guilt, an overwhelming kind of guilt that some-

[1]"There is a green hill far away," C. F. Alexander, 1848.

times leads us either to deny the fact because we cannot bear the terrible truth about ourselves, or to overcompensate with intensive but often unrealistic social action. The pain, the agony, the sweat, the thirst of the cross are all evident in society about us. We know we are involved inextricably in a society that permits these to continue in an age when most basic human needs could be met for the first time in history.

This is hardly *Good* News, even though *true* news. If we can see nothing more in the death of Jesus than our own participation, then we have every right to despair. There is much that is negative about the cross. Is there nothing positive? If the death of Jesus cannot ring an affirming note, there can be nothing but futility to any death. If death has only a negative significance, the whole of life for every man is aimed toward a moment when any value it may have had will be eradicated forever by the grim reaper. "Vanity of vanities! All is vanity" (Ecclesiastes 1:2).

A sharp change in emphasis appeared toward the end of the nineteenth century, though it was by no means readily accepted. P. T. Forsyth heralded this shift when he declared that "the value of the atonement ... does not lie in the suffering at all, but in the obedience...."[2] The negative side of the cross is the terrible suffering it inflicted. That must never be denied. But the positive side is the wonderful obedience and lov-

[2]*The Cruciality of the Cross.* London: Independent Press, 1948, p. 41.

ing self-offering of a lifetime it reveals. Indeed the power of the cross is not directed toward God. Rather it is the power of outpoured love, directed toward mankind. People in every generation have felt the power of that love and their lives in turn have been empowered, upheld, ennobled, made joyous, made significant. "For God so *loved* the world that he gave his only Son, that whoever believes in him should not perish but have eternal life" (John 3:16, emphasis added).

Jesus had established a fellowship between himself and each of his disciples, and their lives had been changed. They found the fellowship among themselves enriched because of their Master. After the initial shock of Good Friday had been overcome by the joy of the Easter event, they knew the fellowship *continued*. Jesus lives! Because he lives, his disciples live. New life has already begun in them. That new life, that resurrected life, is the life of fellowship with a living Savior and Lord. Thus the cross was changed from a disaster to the most profound expression possible of the power of God's love and the strength of fellowship in that love. "Greater love has no man than this, that a man lay down his life for his friends" (John 15:13).

Is it death itself then that brings a spirit of futility, or is it rather the isolated contemplation of death? Impending death is probably a great deal more frightening to the empathetic observer than to the one who is actually dying. An on-

looker is likely to see certain things because of
his own fear of death that the dying man considers irrelevant. One hospital chaplain gives clinical testimony to this in his experience with a
great many dying patients. The four concerns of
the dying, he says, are that (a) he not be alone
but in the company of one or a few persons
whom he loves; (b) he be as free as possible of
pain; (c) he die with dignity rather than in some
grotesque posture or manner; and (d) he deal
satisfactorily with the question, "What happens
to me when I die?" These are the wishes of the
person who is dying. But seldom does the so-
licitous onlooker share these concerns, except
usually the matter of freedom from pain. Few of
these basic concerns were met in Jesus' crucifixion: most of those closest to him deserted him;
he suffered unrelieved agony; he died under the
most grotesque conditions.

Those who looked upon the cross that Good
Friday no doubt saw what their personal perspective enabled them to see. Jewish leaders were re-
lieved at last to be rid of this meddlesome fellow.
Roman soldiers were simply doing their duty.
The disciples were racked with a sense of fear
and failure. Jesus' perspective, the view of the
man actually dying, was quite different. The very
first word he spoke from the cross (the words of a
dying man are terribly important) came as a sur-
prise but also as a clue to the meaning and
power of his death: "Father, forgive. . . ." Jesus'

first concern was to show forth loving forgiveness, to restore and expand his fellowship with mankind. With that word, with that concern, with that offering of love, his dying immediately took on positive overtones, doing at his death what he consistently did in his life, and doing it even more grandly.

4

THE GOOD NEWS OF JESUS CHRIST

The First Problem

"And as for the resurrection of the dead, have you not read what was said to you by God, 'I am the God of Abraham, and the God of Isaac, and the God of Jacob'? He is not God of the dead, but of the living."

Matthew 22:31, 32

One problem in dealing with death—anyone's death—is that we look at it apart from the total life event. We look at death in isolation. The scriptural writers dwell on Jesus' death at great length, but they do it with confidence because they do not separate his death from the *total saving event* of Christ himself. We are conditioned far more by ancient Greek methods of thought than by biblical, so we tend to view life analytically, looking first at its parts. Thus we often miss the forest for the trees, as the saying goes. How indeed do we usually describe the human body? One head, two arms, two legs ... that is the analytical approach. But scriptural writers, grounded in the Hebraic manner of looking at the total picture first, could see parts only as aspects of the whole. Thus they look at the saving event of Christ as a whole: Birth-Life-Death-Descent into Hell-Resurrection-Ascension as one continuing process. It is like a hexagon; separate one of the six sides and you have destroyed not just a side but the very being of the hexagon.

It is difficult, if not impossible, for western minds not to be primarily analytical. For the first three hundred years of the Church's life the Easter event was celebrated as the Great Fifty Days, the Queen of Seasons. Not until the fourth century were divisions made, so that Resurrection was celebrated on Day 1, Ascension on Day 40, and Pentecost on Day 50. The analytical method of examining a subject is certainly important, but we must always remember that the whole is more than the sum of all its parts; its unity is part of its reality, too. Recall the remarkable judgment of King Solomon (1 Kings 3) when the two harlots stood before him, each claiming the same infant as her own. The king demanded that a sword be brought and announced that he would divide the living child in two and give half to each woman. One harlot agreed. But the real mother identified herself when she pleaded with the king not to slay the child but to give it to the other woman. The reality of life is in its unity.

Our failure to behold the unity of our Lord's Life-Death-Life has done serious damage to our understanding of the meaning of his death. By taking his death out of the context of his total and continuing life, we have tended either to dis-

tort it on the one hand, or dismiss it on the
other. But this is not biblical faith. In fact, Paul
could proclaim without any feeling of inconsis-
tency, "For Christ, our paschal lamb, has been
sacrificed. Let us, therefore, *celebrate the
festival . . .*" (1 Corinthians 5:7f, emphasis
added).

So interrelated were death and life in the
hearts of the early, frequently persecuted Christians that by the middle of the second century
they were observing the anniversaries of martyrs
of the faith by celebrating the days of their death.
"For the martyrs were the conspicuous, visible
witnesses to a Christian's full participation with
Christ in death and resurrection. Hence the
Church observed the anniversaries of the deaths
of the martyrs as festive days. . . . In paganism,
anniversaries of birthdays have been observed
—birthdays into the life of this world. In Christianity . . . death was viewed as a 'birthday'
—the birthday into eternity . . . ."[1]

The Good Friday event, therefore, can never
be isolated from what went before—Christ's
birth, his realization of vocation, his ministry
—and from what followed—Christ's descent into
hell (abode of departed spirits), his Resurrection,
his Ascension, his continuing fellowship with
his followers in his Spirit. To separate any aspect of this process of Christ's being is to distort
him, to view him out of context, to miss the posi-

[1]Massey H. Shepherd, Jr., *The Liturgy and the Christian Faith.*
New York: The Seabury Press, 1957, p. 15.

tive thrust of the whole sweep of his nature. We are so accustomed to think of death as the *end* that it takes vigorous effort, requires a new perspective, to see death as a part of the continuation of the fulfilling Christ-event. We see a dead bird and say, "How sad. How beautiful you were. How lovely was your song." The cycle of nature brings fall and then winter. Leaves fall. The fields turn brown. We say, "Another year is over." We feel a bit depressed because it is the end of a span of life never to be recovered. So we are geared by nature and training to look upon human death as the end. Thus we tend to see even the death of Christ as the end.

Until we can break this pattern, we cannot really behold the victory of Christ. There is an absolutely indivisible unity in the Death and Resurrection of our Lord. His death is the victorious march of Christ into the heart of the universe (Descent), into the lives of men (Resurrection), and into the vast cosmos (Ascension). Furthermore, his death follows an earthly life of unparalleled beauty and significance. It is a continuing whole. The saving comes in its entirety. Until we can see Christ's death as the culmination of his earthly life and the beginning of his victory, he can never be to us a Savior, and our own death can be nothing more than the period placed at the end of a sentence.

As we isolate Christ's death and hold it apart from the whole, so we isolate our own or that of one we love. We separate human death; we take it out of context; we box it in—then we ask, "How can I possibly deal with it?" Jeremy Taylor, the seventeenth century Anglican divine, pointed out the day-to-day importance of seeing the unity of life and death. "And indeed since all our life we are dying, ... it is but reasonable, that we should always be doing the offices of preparation. ... as fuel in a furnace in every degree of its heat and reception of the flame is converting into fire and ashes, and the disposing it to the last mutation is the same work with the last instant of its change; so is the age of every day a beginning of death, and the night composing us to sleep bids us go to our lesser rest; because that night which is the end of the preceding day is but a lesser death ... only men are pleased to call that death which is the end of dying, when we cease to die any more. ..."[2]

Death is a stage in the process of life. It is an important and significant stage, to be sure, an anxiety-provoking, painful, determinative stage. It demands our attention; indeed it eventually forces itself upon our attention no matter how we may flee it. It is all consuming. Yet, for the Christian, death is a stage in the process of life,

[2]"Discourse XX. Of death, and the due matter of preparation to it," *The Life of our Blessed Lord and Saviour Jesus Christ*, Part III, Sect. XV, in *The Whole Works of the Right Rev. Jeremy Taylor*, D.D., Vol. II, edited by Reginald Heber and revised by Charles Page Eden. London: Longman, Brown, Green and Longmans, 1850.

life that springs out of a definitive past, life that is called into a purposeful future by a loving God. That is the only perspective by which death can be viewed with appreciation. Death, like birth, is a gateway.

Birth is a gateway into this world when we are no longer attached by any physical cord to that which gave us life. Life does not begin at birth. We do not have to pinpoint the instant in which human reality is there, whether at the moment of conception or at the moment when the fetus is capable of supporting its own life functions—or at some point in between. That argument is unnecessary. The point is that life, human life, does exist, before the contractions that lead to entrance into this world, which we call birth. Thus birth is a gateway from an absolutely dependent life into a new world and a new kind of life, one of developing freedom.

Likewise, Christ reveals that in him death is also a gateway, the transition from a semifree or at times oppressive world into an absolutely free one, the transition from relative dependence to independence, from a limited life to an open one. If the fetus could reason shortly before its birth, no doubt it would have great anxiety about what lies ahead. How comfortable and warm and controlled the womb is. Why would anyone want to leave it for another kind of existence? Yet, if the leaving were not accomplished, growth and development would reach a plateau beyond which it could not go. Birth is necessary. One must pass through the gate so that life can become enlarged, so that personhood can develop, with all the restrictions of the womb left behind.

Death is like that. What is our Lord's Ascension all about if not the proclamation that his life can never again be identified with merely one spot, one moment in history. He is universal. He has the freedom of his being that early, human confinement would never permit. The gateway of death opened into a new and free life for him, the opportunity for fellowship with all people, in all places, in all times. His promise is that he is preparing this kind of life for us, "that where I am you may be also" (John 14:3).

Truly the goal of Christian life is to grow through life and death and life again in continuing and eternal communion with Christ. The amount of time—whether great or small—spent at any stage along the way, therefore, achieves its importance only from being a part of the total continuing process. My wife and I wrestled through this when our twin sons died shortly after birth. Is the duration of life in this world a decisive factor in the development of eternal life? Absolutely not. What more can parents desire for their children than a continuing relationship with their Savior and growth in his love? Parents yearn for companionship with their children and mourn any deprivation of it. Yet whether earthly

life be a few days, or a few years, or three score
and ten, when that life is seen in the context of
progressive growth through death and resurrection in Christ, the joy of faith shines through the
tears of sorrow.

> For everything there is a season, and a time
> for every matter under heaven:
>> a time to be born, and a time to die;
>> a time to plant, and a time to pluck up what
>> is planted ...
>> a time to weep, and a time to laugh;
>> a time to mourn, and a time to dance ...
>> a time to seek, and a time to lose;
>> a time to keep, and a time to cast away; ...
>>> Ecclesiastes 3:1,2,4,6

Yet all these times are within the overarching
providence and love of God.

For Jesus, death was the necessary conclusion to earthly life, as it is the necessary conclusion to ours. But for Jesus, death was not defeat,
the abrupt ending of what could have been a
beautiful story. Jesus' death was a positive action, a bringing to focus of what he was in his
earthly life, a transition point in his total ministry to us. Death was the next step in the continuing Birth-Life-Death-Descent-Resurrection-
Ascension *event* that made Jesus unique and effectively changed the possibilities for everyone
who follows him. No longer do we have to look
upon death, whenever it comes, as the final cur-

tain on this production. Rather, it is Scene I of the next act of life in Jesus Christ.

5

THE GOOD NEWS OF JESUS CHRIST

The Second Problem

"You shall love the Lord your God with all your heart, and with all your soul, and with all your mind. This is the great and first commandment. And a second is like it, You shall love your neighbor as yourself."

Matthew 22:37-39

A second problem is equally troublesome in facing death and our Lord with real hope. This is our tendency to try to live spiritually as individuals, apart from any community, devoid of close spiritual ties. It is *my* life and *my* death about which I am essentially concerned. Yet the truth is that we share life—and death—with every other human being. What is equally important is that we also share with others—or fail to share—our faith, our trust in our Lord and Savior.

New life comes into being not from individual action or will but through two other lives. Thus, immediately there is the basis for community: father, mother, child. Life requires a community to be sustained. A newborn infant is most vulnerable. He must have warmth and food and care. Behavioral sciences point out strongly how essential love is even with the very youngest. The need to be loved is quite as great as any physical need. Without love, an infant will shortly become physically or emotionally deformed, or even die, no matter how adequately nourished.

Further, we must live in community in order to develop into whole people. A hermit condition will inevitably result in distortion of personality. The natural need and tendency for community is exaggerated today as our cities grow larger but less personal and the vast rural areas become sparser in population. A child today must have the care not only of his parents but also of untold numbers of other persons, known and unknown to him, to develop the personality and skills required to live successfully in these times. No one comes into this world of his own volition; no one achieves maturity with his own resources alone; no one can accurately or honestly call himself a "self-made" person.

Likewise, our faith is not a private possession. We are the inheritors of the centuries and the beneficiaries of those contemporary people of faith who have introduced us to our Lord and nurtured us in his love. This is as God has planned it. The Spirit of God comes not so much to one person as he does in the midst of two or three gathered together in Christ's name. My birth into the Christian community through the Spirit of God in Baptism came through the actions of a minister and a congregation. I cannot receive Holy Communion alone, but only in company with other faithful souls. True, I can pray and meditate and study alone—and do. Yet I am not really alone. My prayers continually focus about others; the Bible I study is the Word of God coming through the lives and writings of others; I may even be sitting or kneeling in a chapel planned and built by others, and cleaned today by still another.

When our Lord proclaimed for us the Divine Commandment of love for God, neighbor, and self, he was not giving us a "law to end laws." He was not bequeathing to us a lovely rule, an "ought," that if lived by would bring peace and happiness to all. The genius of his bringing together these two Old Testament affirmations was in his proclamation that the essence of a whole, integrated, developed, mature self can evolve only in a *caring community*. Love for God, for fellowman, and for self is not just a beautiful ideal. Entering into the process of realizing it is entering into God's continuing creation. It is sharing his life; it is fulfilling one's own life.

We need one another. We need the supportive concern we can offer one another. I have come to realize that the little widow who greets

me after service on Sunday morning with the
question, "Did you miss me while I was away?"
is not merely passing the time of day. In her
aloneness, she needs to be missed. She really
needs to be loved within the community—and
the minister, for that moment, is the symbol of
that community and that love. The minister himself is in the same boat. He needs to be needed.
The one concern you can be sure every person
has the moment you meet him is his need to be
accepted by you. This may be disguised in vari-
ous ways. He may want "to impress you," "to
come across favorably." Or in his fear of the pain
of rejection, he may hold back and prevent a real
meeting from taking place. But this, too, is evidence of his underlying need for loving concern.

Our ability to accept ourselves in a healthy
fashion and to feel good about ourselves is
greatly determined by the way other people treat
us. If people think of me as kind, I tend to think
of myself in the same manner. If they think I am
mean, I will tend to agree. My own self-image is
largely drawn from how others react to me. If I
am sought after, I am happy; if I am ignored, I
am dejected.

There is a great deal of talk today about our
need for love; much of it is sentimental, maud-
lin, and unreal. Perhaps it would be better to say
that we need to be affirmed by others, for certainly the opposite of love is not hate but

indifference. If you hate me and display it, you are still paying attention to me. There are those who thrive on just such unhealthy attention. But if you refuse to show in any way that I even exist, I am a nobody. True personal affirmation is not always complimentary. It must always be honest. The most honest thing a concerned person can do for me is to disagree when he knows I am wrong, to become angry with me when I refuse to care for him, to refuse to accept less of me than the best I can offer. There is nothing saccharine about this kind of loving concern. I must have supportive concern, and if not that, then at least your attention—or I cease to be; death has indeed begun.

Thus fear of death is closely allied with fear of the loss of the love, the support, that makes us what we are, that holds us together, that propels us into life with courage and joy. It has been said that "suicide is the death of love." The loss of love, the resulting sense of worthlessness, is death. Everyone has a taste of this at one time or another. "Life is not worth living," we say. We need strong support at such a moment; we need an upholding hand; we need a loving community. Indeed, we need such a supportive community at all times.

A healthy respect for ourselves is nurtured by a caring family and community, but no family or community can be continuously caring without the refining love of Jesus Christ. Human love by itself tends to want to possess, to hold on to and thus limit another person. Human love must reflect ultimately the love of God or it will degenerate into enslavement and weakness. How many groups have begun with high ideals of human love! How few have lasted. The knowledge and experience of God's love alone can make love for our fellowman and for ourselves honest and real. Without a source beyond ourselves, love loses direction, turns to selfishness, lacks the security to risk itself for others, tries to hold on and dominate. The ultimate source of honest caring lies outside ourselves. It is at this point that even the most idealistic humanism invariably fails. Our Lord established a special community within which the Spirit of God can be known and experienced, can renew the life and love of its members. This community was established to provide support for its members as together they receive support from God; and in turn to extend love to others outside the household of faith. This, at its best, is what the parish church is called to be, what any group of Christians, and especially the Christian family, is called to be.

Since the Spirit of God operates most effectively in the midst of the community of faith, the tendency to individualism, whether in faith or practice, weakens our faith because it weakens the community in which the love of Jesus Christ is made real to us. It is necessary for us to have this supportive community to experience the continuing process of growth in the life of Christ. Only in such a context can we really look at death as a step in that process, not fearing to follow our Lord in the path he has already marked for us. The hospital chaplain who observed that the first need of the dying patient is loving companionship was verifying the essential need for love that makes the difference between death in the context of life and life ended in death.

Significantly, the last thing Jesus did before he went out to die was to fix the meaning of his death and of what was to follow from it upon the minds of his followers. He established in that Last Supper of fellowship the Holy Eucharist, which immediately became the focal point of the Christian community at worship. It is in fact a recalling of his *death*. "For as often as you eat this bread and drink the cup, you proclaim the Lord's death until he comes" (1 Corinthians 11:26).

The Eucharist at its best is never a somber occasion but rather, as the word "eucharist" means, a *thanksgiving,* a joyous celebration of a death that is the means to life. Jesus' death was positive rather than negative, a movement ahead rather than a return to zero, an affirmation rather than a destruction. It was all this because it was essentially a sacramental action.

Not by chance has the liturgical pattern of

Christian worship consistently manifested a
form, a structure, always identifiable in the actions of Offering, Consecration, and Communion; for these are the deepest, most significant
actions of life. In the celebration of the
Eucharist, the sacrament of Christ's death, Christians have always found the channel to his life.
In offering the liturgy we indeed are participat-
ing in the very life—and in the very process of
that life that turns death into triumph and the
means to life everlasting. Eucharistic living and
dying is the means of growing in fellowship with
Christ, without which we are already dead re-
gardless of how much vitality we may exhibit.
Eucharistic living enables us to enter into the
whole of our Lord's life and see as a whole our
own life and death and life again. Eucharistic living enables us to grow in a continuing supportive community that nourishes our trust and our
hope. Indeed, in eucharistic living and dying we
become ourselves a sacrament of promise and
hope.

6

EUCHARISTIC LIVING/DYING

The Offering: Part A

*"And this is eternal life, that they know
thee the only true God, and Jesus Christ
whom thou hast sent."*

John 17:3

"What happens to you has to be borne, and how
you bear it is more important than what it is
—more important than how it comes out." These
are the last written words of a woman dying of
cancer, scribbled with a failing hand, found
shortly after her death by her husband. They are
both her final testament and her personal encouragement to him.

She had suffered for nearly four years: chem-
ical therapy, radio-therapy, surgery—hope and
despair and hope again. Through it all there was
a wonderful openness, a refusal to hide or disguise the truth. There was an openness to her
husband and children; and there was an open-

ness with God through daily prayer and Bible
study and regular receiving of Holy Communion
and the Laying on of Hands. While the body
weakened, the spirit grew.

Christian faith is not based on a vain hope
for the "immortality of the soul." There is no assurance that anything within us, in and of itself,
possesses the quality of survival beyond death. It
was the ancient Greek philosopher Plato who
contributed this idea to mankind, and somehow
it has picked up almost biblical credibility. It is
not biblical. New Testament insight attributes
nothing to the human being that guarantees
eternal survival.

What the New Testament affirms very
strongly, however, is the eternal value that God
himself places upon every person, a value so
great he is willing to offer his only Son to open
an everlasting relationship with himself. Thus
what a person can possess, not through his own
innate worth or his personal good works but as
God's gift, is *fellowship with his living Lord.* It is
that fellowship which nothing, not even death,
can destroy. As Paul affirms in his letter to the
Church in Rome: "He who did not spare his own
Son but gave him up for us all, will he not also
give us all things with him? . . . For I am sure
that neither death, nor life, nor angels, nor principalities, nor things present, nor things to come,
nor powers, nor height, nor depth, nor anything
else in all creation, will be able to separate us

from the love of God in Christ Jesus our Lord"
(8:32, 38f).

My indissoluble (except by me) communion
with Christ is my assurance of life that continues
through death. Because he lives—and because
through my response to his invitation I live in
him—I will continue to live with him. "It is not
the intrinsic quality of my soul nor something
supposedly immortal within me that brings me
through. No, it is this Wanderer who marches at
my side as Lord and Brother and who can no
more abandon me on the other side than he
could let me out of his hand here on this side of
the grave."[1]

Personal fellowship with Christ is greatly
dependent upon personal fellowship with others
in Christ, what Scripture calls "the fellowship of
the Holy Spirit." There is a distinct difference
between "personal religion" and "individualism." Personal religion always involves
other people. Involvement with other Christians,
through which our life with Christ is nourished,
can develop only as we are prepared to take the
risks that personal relationships always involve.
The willingness to take the risk, to share, to ex-
pose ourselves to hurt as well as support—this is
the beginning of the Offertory of our lives, the
point at which our life and our death become
sacramental, the outward and visible signs of a

[1]Helmut Thielicke, *Death and Life*. Philadelphia: Fortress Press,
1970, p. xxvi.

deepening quality of life and growing communion with our Lord.

"This *is* eternal life. . . ." To know God and Jesus, to enter into relationship with our Lord, *is* eternal life *now*. This is when it begins, at the offering, an offering that must continue day after day until at last it is accepted at God's eternal altar. But it is not the final goal alone that motivates us, for communion with Christ gives new life now, with new horizons and new meaning and new joy and new direction. "We're not just concerned with everlastingness, just endlessness. We are concerned with that; but we're concerned more with a new quality of life that begins now and lasts forever. It's a fellowship with God and with one another that gives meaning and power to life now. And actually what we want to do in the church is to move people from little lives to great lives, and to give the glory back to life which God meant it to have."[2]

It is the wonderfully loving self-offering of a lifetime that attracts us so strongly to our Lord. The cross was not something sprung on him unexpectedly. It loomed before him throughout his ministry and before. The struggles of Jesus were not limited to the physical pains of his Passion. We are aware of some of his inner wrestlings, from the Temptations, on which, significantly, are described for us immediately after the

[2]Richard S. Emrich, *Death and Hope*. Cincinnati, Ohio: Forward Movement Publications, undated, p. 21.

launching of his public ministry at his baptism by John. The temptations themselves are clearly struggles that plagued him again and again, brought to a focus finally in the Garden of Gethsemane the night he was betrayed. Calvary was the outward and visible sign of suffering and triumph already achieved in his inner life of wrestling in prayer. The event on Calvary was the summation of his life, the visible expression of a consistent inward battle as he worked out the implications of his relationship with his Father. One physician says, "... the so-called agony of dying is really the culmination of the agony of living; it occurred before the struggle was over, before dying had begun. The agony of Jesus was in Gethsemane, not on the Cross. From this it appears that the agony of dying begins at birth. . . ."[3]

Death is not an isolated event but rather it is inextricably involved with the life of which it is a part. Nor is it only the moment that closes earthly existence. Death is an ongoing condition and possibility at every moment. So Paul could proclaim of himself, "as dying, and behold we live" (2 Corinthians 6:9). What took place in the Garden of Gethsemane and then was acted out on Calvary was not an isolated crisis; it was the focus of a lifelong temptation and of a lifelong victory over temptation. It was in a divine fellow-

[3]Paul Gibson, M.D., "The Agony of Dying," *Frontier*, 4:3, Winter 1960, p. 283.

ship finally realized that Jesus could approach
Good Friday with trust and confidence.

That struggle began for Jesus in the first
moments of his self-awareness, as it does for
every person. For the agony of the Garden really
began in another Garden at the dawn of religious
history. It is the agony that is involved in praying
honestly, "Not my will but thine . . ." when all
the time the internal pressure is saying, "No!
Not thy will but *mine.*" The agony lies in facing
the truth of all creation: real life, real power, real
freedom can come only in accepting God's fellowship and offering our fellowship in turn to
him and to his children. Real life comes only
through death. Willingness to risk ourselves in
fellowship comes only as our self-centeredness
begins to die. It is a painful and lifelong dying
and everyone shrinks from it. Yet the only alter-
native is a decision for selfishness, and this
brings death, too, a destructive death, because we
have refused to affirm a goodness and source of
power beyond our own—we have refused to live.
Is this not what the theologians really mean
when they speak of "mortal sin"? There are thus
two kinds of death possible for every person:
"self-destroying" death and "self-affirming"
death. Our only real choice lies in how we are
going to proceed.

Jesus' death had to come some time in his
earthly life. He was truly man, and man must die

eventually. The question was, how should it come? Should it come to one seeking to flee life in frantic efforts at self-preservation ("self-destroying"), or to one ready to face life in full self-offering ("self-affirming")? Jesus obviously chose the latter. He chose it again and again, at every step of his life. He chose it eventually when he decided to go up to Jerusalem, the beginning of the journey that led by Gethsemane and Calvary to the right hand of God. But it had to be his choice, his decision, his own affirmation. He could make the awesome final choice because he had made it repeatedly in fellowship with a Father he knew and trusted.

Every man enters death alone. Even if he is going down on a fiery airplane with a hundred other people aboard, he is entering death alone. Dr. Thielicke likens death to the platform gate at the railroad depot. "Only one at a time can pass through, and above it stand the words: 'Your life is nontransferable. Now it is you alone who are on the spot; for you the end has come.' "[4] Though it is a lonely moment for a person, it is also the moment of profound self-affirmation, completely free of sham and pretense, free of pressures from others, free of the limitations and demands of the body, of the dermal sheath that has surrounded and confined him since his creation. No longer is he restricted from being his real self. In death a person ex-

[4]Op. cit., p. xxii.

periences his first moment of *absolute* freedom,
freedom to assert finally and ultimately what he
has tried weakly to assert before: that he is in
communion with his Savior, or that he refuses
such communion. Nothing else matters. Nothing
else is involved. The relationship one has been
choosing and developing can now take on everlasting proportions.

Thus the moment of death becomes a
person's final offering, the moment of full encounter with God. It is at the moment of death
that one makes his ultimate response to God's
love, and in that response one at last reaches the
fullness of his humanity. We see Jesus facing
that moment himself. The struggle had been
there all the while, Satan beckoning this way and
that, often so vividly it was difficult to distinguish between his way and God's, between "my
will" and "thine." So out of the travail of his
soul Jesus lifted up his eyes to God and commit-
ted himself absolutely to him. "Father, glorify
thy name." In that moment the crisis of the ages
was reached; in that moment every man's destiny
was laid bare in the glory of God's love.

We look upon death quite naturally as the
real dividing point in a person's existence. What
happens before death is observable, measurable,
and real. What happens after death—if
anything—is mysterious and unknowable. This
is such a natural view that we often assume it is
what the New Testament teaches. On the con-

trary, the New Testament asserts that the real dividing point in a person's life is not his physical death but the moment of inner awareness when he really begins to respond positively to our Lord's invitation to fellowship, the moment at which his sacramental baptism into the death of Christ (if it has already occurred) becomes a *volitional reality,* when he responds to God's expression of love and summons to follow Christ with a sincere "I will," or at least, "I want to." The eternal value of that fellowship with our Lord is in his promise, ". . . whoever lives and believes in me shall never die" (John 11:26).

Christianity is not a set of beliefs—even belief in life-through-death—which a person must somehow bring himself to accept before he qualifies as a member of the Christian church. A man's Christianity becomes vital, his faith becomes real, when he begins living on the resources of God, recognizing that God in Christ has a claim on his life, and giving priority to that claim in everything he is. When that happens to a person, he usually makes a startling discovery. He no longer asks about the necessity of believing in life after death, because his experience of life in Christ is such that he must believe it goes on forever. He has already entered into a new phase of being, the new resurrection order of "life in Christ" in which death opens new possibilities. It was in such an awareness that Paul could reveal his own dilemma, "My desire is to depart and be with Christ, for that is far better. But to remain in the flesh is more necessary on your account" (Philippians 1:23b, 24).

Our initial response to God in Jesus Christ, whenever and however it comes, is the beginning of self-affirmation. It is the beginning of the "offertory of life," the holding up of our lives to God, which permits God to take the raw substance of our limited being and transform us into living creatures of his eternity. Death still lies ahead, to be sure; but it becomes the "outward sign" of our initial response and the innumerable responses throughout our earthly life when there has been a "dying" to our old natures and a "rising" to newness of life. It is that final moment of the greatest and freest self-affirmation as "a member of Christ, the child of God, and an inheritor of the kingdom of heaven" (*The Book of Common Prayer*, p. 283). Death focuses for us the essentially sacramental nature of life when what we offer to God—no matter how weakly —he accepts and ennobles and perfects for that wonderful and everlasting encounter with him.

7

EUCHARISTIC LIVING/DYING

The Offering: Part B

*"So if you are offering your gift at the altar, and
there remember that your brother has something against
you, leave your gift there before the altar and go;
first be reconciled to your brother, and then come and
offer your gift."*

Matthew 5:23-24

It is one thing to look at the earthly life of Jesus
Christ culminating in his death upon the cross
as a total act of offering himself to God and for
God; it is quite another to look at my own life in
that way. How can I possibly view my life and
my eventual death as an act of "offering" to
God? I was baptized before I knew what was
going on. I can remember my Confirmation. The
bishop came. It was raining that day and my hair
was wet. I was concerned that the bishop would
get his hands wet when he laid them on my
head! I do believe in God—and in Jesus Christ
as his Son. I worship God from time to time. I
have a conscience. I believe God will take care
of me. But most of the time I don't think of God.
I simply cannot consider my life as a conscious

"offering" to him that I present in myself at the moment of death.

This is an honest and totally expected response and reservation. Most Christians just do not think of themselves—or want to think of themselves—in quite so saintly a role. I respond to this reservation in terms of that first problem we invariably have upon hearing the Good News, which we discussed in Chapter Four. Not only do we look upon our Lord's life as a sequence of events, we also take a "snapshot" approach to our own life, life that can realistically be viewed only as a continuing moving picture, an ongoing process that sums up all that has gone before and points toward all that will happen in the future. We have already seen the difficulties we encounter when we isolate one aspect of our Lord's life and bring our attention to focus solely on that bit without proper balance with the rest. There is only *one* event really; that is the Christ-event: his Birth-Life - Death - Descent - Resurrection - Ascension and, we should properly add, his Coming Again. The same is true for every child of God. We create impossible problems for ourselves by isolating moments, holding them up for examination, and not seeing all our moments as inseparable from the entirety of life.

Churchmen, for example, conjure up all kinds of difficulties for themselves by distorting the process of Baptism through which each member of the Church is given "life in the

Spirit," incorporated into the Body of Jesus Christ, and grafted into the community of believers. We regularly fail to distinguish between "Baptism: the process of new life" and "Baptism: the sacramental rite."

It is in the rite itself that the baptismal process is summarized and capsulated, to be sure; but clearly Baptism is not an instantaneous event that is then done with. It is a *process*, brought to a focus in that sacramental moment and launched into all the moments that lie ahead. Thus, for every Christian the baptismal process is still going on—and will continue to go on —just as in a physical birth the significance is in the new life rather than in the birth-event itself. Unless the new life continues to grow into the fullness of its selfhood, the birth-event is of minor or even tragic significance.

Traditional theology makes a clear distinction between "regeneration" in Baptism, on the one hand, and "conversion," on the other. Regeneration, or "new life," is given as an act of God whether the recipient is aware of it or not. Conversion, however, is the conscious turning of the individual soul to God, a process that can come before Baptism, long after, or even, never.

In Baptism we receive the gift of the Holy Spirit, by which we mean God's grace, his power living and working within us. The early Church Fathers speak of "prevenient grace," the touch of God's Spirit that comes before the awareness of his presence, the unseen hand that leads people to God in the first place. Everyone is surrounded, indeed was created and is now being upheld by God's Spirit, whether he recognizes him or not. When such a person responds to God's presence, either through the faithful witness of family and friends or through undiscernible forces, in a deliberate manner so that the gift of the Spirit becomes his in Baptism, then we see that the process of life in Christ, while brought to a viable focus in the sacrament, really began with the beginning of the individual life itself. Thus we have to think of the baptismal process in three distinct phases: (a) the prelude by which a person is led by the Spirit to Baptism in Christ; (b) the beginning of new life in Christ given through the administration of the sacrament itself; and (c) the continuing growth of the regenerate person toward the ultimate unity with Jesus Christ that is of the nature of heaven.

Thus one is not "offering" himself to Christ by walking about as though a halo were already in place. The prayer in the baptismal rite states it well when we ask of the Holy Spirit "that those who here are cleansed from sin may be born again, and continue for ever in the risen life of Jesus Christ our Savior...."[1] We continue to live our lives as human beings but in the pres-

---

[1] *Services for Trial Use,* Authorized Alternatives to Prayer Book Services (Episcopal). New York: The Church Hymnal Corporation, 1971, p. 28.

ence and with the power and love of the risen
Christ. I am sure our Lord would feel we were
shirking our duty if we thought about him all the
time. We one-track-minded people must think
about our families and our jobs and about the
hundred and one little things that, rightly, oc-
cupy us in this world. Jesus is not jealous because I give my full attention for a bit to replac-
ing a windowpane! Doing it as well as I can for
the benefit of home and family—and self-
satisfaction—is surely a part of the offering of my
life. I become who I am by living out my life in
the particular context in which I find myself.
That, in essence, is my offering just as it was
Jesus' offering before me.

There are, of course, certain disciplines that
I must undertake, indeed that I will want to undertake, to assure that living out my life in my
particular context also involves growth in Christ.
Worship in the community of faith is absolutely
essential for me to maintain and develop a truly
Christian perspective and to experience personal
affirmation as a Christian. Personal and family
prayer on a regular basis are necessary. Bible
study, with some guide or help, is critical if I am
to become established within the tradition of
faith. Some reaching out of myself to others, outside my family and church, in the name of Christ
is necessary for my growth. It is not popular
today to talk about discipline; but it strikes me
that the people I know are very hungry indeed

for a meaningful framework for their lives, for a truly spiritual discipline.

There still arises concern for "the - poor - native - in-the-heart - of- darkest-Africa" who has never heard of Jesus Christ, that hypothetical individual who has undoubtedly had more sympathy and received less benefit than any other of God's children! The real root of this concern often lies near to the one who expresses it. He is really interested either in himself or in someone quite close to him who, he feels, simply doesn't measure up. "Uncle Harry was as good a man as ever lived, but one would never know that he ever had a thought about God." "I worked for years to get my poor husband interested in church; but he just never would respond—and now he is dead."

What about "Uncle Harry" and the widow's unresponsive husband? They did not think of life as an "offering." They made no apparent effort in that direction. They led reasonably good lives, cared for their families, departed this life as respectable citizens. Or, perhaps, one or the other was not really respectable or highly moral. What about them?

It is natural that we should be concerned about those for whom we care who, quite simply, do not meet our Christian expectations. Yet we must be very careful in evaluating another man's life. "Judge not" is a direct command of our Lord, and we had best pay strict heed to it. God alone is the one "unto whom all hearts are open, all desires known, and from whom no secrets are hid" (*The Book of Common Prayer,* p. 67). He has revealed the depth of his love and mercy in the cross of his Son. We know that even the judgment of God is not for the purpose of vindicating his honor but rather for the perfecting of his children. Anxiety about other people's records will not help them, but our continuing prayers very well may. Our purpose is not to make an estimate of any other man's life but rather to provide a structure by which a man can look at his own life and either begin or continue to build toward a destiny that is both positive and hopeful, toward which God is now calling him. I am convinced that the Lord Jesus Christ who offered his very life for every man does not rest content with our evangelistic efforts alone. Who can tell what response another man has made, or when? Did not a thief upon his cross open the door of faith? We must not be sentimental about this, for certainly God respects our ultimate choice. As Professor Thielicke has remarked, the idea of universal salvation is a "gospel for playboys." At the same time we must not underestimate the saving love of Jesus Christ. Nor must we spare any effort to demonstrate to our neighbor the reality of God's love for him.

So let us look again at ourselves, for it is through our response now that the offering of ourselves is taking place. This offering is the essential first step that makes the difference, the following in the way Christ has led, for death has been transformed by him—even in its horror —from the tragic conclusion of life "into the advent of God in the midst of that empty loneliness, into the manifestation of a complete, obedient surrender of the whole man to the Holy God at the very moment when man seems lost and far removed from him."[2] What a contrast between the confession of Hobbes the skeptic, "I am going to take a leap into the dark—I commit my body to the worms and my spirit to the great Perhaps," and the confession of Paul, "For to me to live is Christ, and to die is gain" (Philippians 1:21).

The event of the death of Jesus did not begin on Calvary, or before Pilate, or even in Gethsemane. The event of the death of Jesus began at his birth. Death is a present reality in every life. So the question becomes not *whether* we shall die but, rather, *how* shall we experience our death? Shall we run from it until it catches us at last, like hunted rabbits, and finishes us; or shall we offer our living and our dying to God as Jesus did before us? Destruction—or affirmation? Jesus has shown us that there can be no real life without running the risk of pain and death, without self-offering. If we withdraw from the dangers of life, we become freaks, a living death.

[2]Karl Rahner, *On the Theology of Death*, No. 2 in *Quaestiones Disputatae*. New York: The Seabury Press, 1962, p. 78.

The essence of living, then, is personal offering, encountering others, running the risks of pain and death because that is the only way life rises above mere animal existence. Indeed, as many have pointed out, opening up our existence to meet another person creates our real being —our "being with" that person. There is no meaningful understanding of self apart from relationships with others.

This self-offering, running the risks of pain and death, is the real manifestation of love. The best love stories usually end in death, because love is itself death. Only in dying to self for the sake of others can arise the total surrender that is love at its finest.

In that greatest love story of all—greatest because it is true for every person—death is the culminating focus. By his perfect self-offering, by his perfect love for us "even to death" (Matthew 26:38), Christ has unleashed the work of salvation upon the world. Death is not the shameful end, but the affirmation of a victory won through obedience, through *offering,* which is the first, the necessary, the crucial act of a sacramental life, a life that fully encounters God.

8

EUCHARISTIC LIVING/DYING

The Consecration: Part A

"He said, 'It is finished'; and he bowed his head and gave up his spirit."

John 19:30

The offertory in our personal lives is the process in which we consciously and deliberately begin to perceive and respond to God's love for us. Making this offering is a lifelong process. For many of us it is tentatively made, withdrawn, made again, throughout our conscious life, and the final decision is not made absolutely until the moment of absolute freedom, the moment of death itself. Thus, the moment of death becomes the consecration, the accomplishment, the fulfillment of the offering of life—not the end of life. So Jesus, nearing the end of the last moments of his earthly consciousness could say, "It is finished." He certainly did not mean that life was all over, that he was washed up, through. Rather, he meant, "It is now accomplished. What I came to do is done. My life has at last been brought to an absolute focus upon God. Here it is!" The manhood of Christ had done all that flesh and

blood could do. He had been responsive, obedient, even to the death upon the cross, and his
very obedience now made God's consecration
of his life possible. Indeed, death itself for
Jesus was the ultimate witness to his complete
obedience to God.

Death is the point at which every person
can finally and fully commit himself to God,
the point at which God himself lovingly takes
over. You make your ultimate response. God
does the rest. Your own free self-affirmation
achieves in death absolute determination. God
ratifies a person's choice for all eternity.

Thus death is both a dreadful and a joyous
event. It often appears to be the instant of absolute loneliness, when one stands spiritually
naked, defenseless. We have only what we have
become until that moment. We have our response to our Lord's love, but it is often weak,
tentative. There can be no sham, no disguise.
Yet at the same time, it is the instant of fulfillment; in death we behold the love of God
ready to receive us as we are, to enfold us, to
form us into the new beings of his eternal
kingdom.

On the cross Jesus revealed both of these
moments as his death approached. "My God,
my God, why hast thou forsaken me?" (Mark
15:34). Though this was quoted directly from
Psalm 22, it found vocal expression on his
weakened lips as no other verse did. It contains all the destitution of his agony, his abject
loneliness, the questioning, even the anger and

depression at why it had to be this way, the struggle against the absolute emptiness in facing death. But the agony gave way to the calm of achievement and trust at the very moment at which his consciousness slipped away; for as the last ounce of his life ebbed from his body, he bowed his head and said, "Father, into thy hands I commit my spirit!" (Luke 23:46).

The physical and emotional responses in a dying person are often quite similar to the dying pangs of our Lord recorded in the Gospels. Professor Joseph Bancroft conducted an experiment by placing himself at the very threshold of death. Under surveillance in a refrigerated room, he sat shivering, flexed limbs huddling up, very conscious of the cold, until almost the end when he relaxed in a beautiful feeling of warmth. He describes this feeling of the moment just before the death process would begin in him as one of "basking" in warmth. "The reactions he records are all to be explained as the attempt of the body to maintain the temperature of the circulating blood at its normal level. . . . When the overwrought body abandoned the struggle, all suffering vanished with a blissful sense of release."[1]

In a less clinical way we can observe a similar response in the person of advanced age who has "given up the fight," who has "lost the will to live," who in short is both ready

[1]Paul Gibson, "The Agony of Dying," *Frontier*, Vol. 4, No. 3, Winter 1961, p. 238.

and eager for death. It is most certainly not a
suicidal impulse. Such a person has often
"fought the good fight" of life with courage for
many years. Now there is great weariness, loss
of most feeling and awareness of the world. He
may have become almost like an infant in the
crib, yet without the potential for growth and
development. There is a relaxation about it all.
"I am ready," he often says. Nearly always
death comes very shortly.

As we seek to describe the moment of death,
one point needs to be clarified. The Bible does
not look at a person as a "body-plus-soul," a de-
tachable combination temporarily hooked up like
two space vehicles in the same orbit, waiting to
undock at the moment of death. We have discussed earlier the problem we experience because
we tend by training to follow the ancient Greek
analytical manner of looking at reality, that is,
looking at the parts. Jewish thought, however,
tends to look at the whole as a unity. "Today
practically every psychologist agrees with the
Bible on this issue. When we talk wisely of
psychosomatic medicine or trace a person's dis-
position to the activity of his glands, we are
doing (with more or less scientific precision)
what the Bible writers did intuitively. In Christian history, Augustine did the same thing when
he said, in words that all our modern knowledge
vindicates, 'For the body is not an extraneous
ornament or aid, but a part of man's very

nature.' "[2]

The importance of emphasizing body/soul as one indivisible entity is seen as well in our readiness to accept another Greek philosophical concept, the natural immortality of the soul. It bears repeating that this is not biblical understanding at all. Yet it has become so familiar in popular thought that many Christians today take it as doctrine! The ancient Greek idea is that the soul is in truth a tiny fragment of the Universal Soul (or God), imprisoned for a time in an earthly body. The aim of that soul is to become free of the decaying body and return to and be absorbed in the Universal Soul. Thus the soul is naturally immortal because it is a part of the immortal Universal Soul. At the same time, it lacks any kind of personal identity. Further, "immortal" implies *pre*-existence to this life as well as continuing existence beyond this earthly life, while the Christian idea of "everlasting life" implies a life with a temporal beginning which by God's grace continues on in his eternity. For the New Testament, the life that a man has beyond death is dependent upon the life and fellowship he has in Jesus Christ. Just as that life we have now is his gift to us, so also is that new, resurrected life in him. In the New Testament it is impossible to draw sharp distinctions between "body" and "soul" or "spirit." "Body" refers to the total per-

[2]Roger L. Shinn, *Life, Death, and Destiny.* Philadelphia: The Westminster Press, 1957, p. 83.

son, which includes all that he is. "Soul" can mean vitality or life, the essence of personhood. So the image of the soul of a dying person floating off to heaven like the helium from a child's punctured balloon is absolutely foreign to Scripture.

At this point the question arises naturally about the significance of the "resurrection of the body." This conviction is an integral part of our faith, proclaimed in our creeds. How are we going to deal with the problem of separation of body and soul at death? Clearly the physical body does die; that cannot be denied. Is the disembodied soul, which would then be something less than a person, put in "cold storage," so to speak, for an indefinite stay, waiting for the end of time, the Second Coming, when the dead shall be raised?

The problem, it seems to me, is basically one of chronology, of the sequence of time, conditioned by our inability to adopt God's eternal viewpoint. Just as death is a factor in our being from our very birth, not solely at the end of our earthly existence, so we create our own problem by thinking of personal resurrection as something that happens instantly at that moment at the end of time when Christ returns in triumph. It is not inconsistent with Scripture, and it is far easier to handle, to consider personal resurrection as beginning *before* death as in faith we "put on the Lord Jesus Christ." Why should we think of

resurrection as instantaneous? Every other aspect
of our life requires growth and is progressive.
Resurrection is the giving of new life and a new
life expression (a "spiritual body" in Paul's
necessarily contradictory phrase) to the total
"me." The giving of this new life and form can
best be thought of as a *process* that comes about
as a person commits himself to God in Christ, a
process that continues until perfection, the ultimate fruition of creation, the General Resurrection, when Christ offers all creation made perfect
to his Father. Indeed, if we are to be consistent,
the resurrection process began at our Baptism,
when we were united with the risen life of
Christ. Christian living in this world is in reality
the process of spiritualizing human life. Death
frees the personality to take up the new life and
form that he chose long before. So it is that the
seed of the "spiritual body" is alive in the Christian even now (see 1 Corinthians 15:35-50).

While we cannot really picture the reality of
"eternity," it is helpful to look at it symbolically.
I see history—man's history, a nation's history,
my history, any history—as a straight line with a
beginning and an end. I can put dates on that
line, at least beginning dates, and I know there
will be final ones. God's eternity I visualize as a
perfect sphere far larger in diameter than any
line of history but enveloping that line, enfolding
it, giving it dimensions it cannot have alone.

Every point on that line is surrounded by eternity. Every point on that line, every moment in my life, is in direct contact with the fullness and completeness of God's being. I live now in eternity, but I can experience only hints of it until I come to that end point on my historical line and God takes me by the hand for the step into his eternal kingdom.

In the same way we can deal with the Second Coming of Christ. Christ is the goal of that historical line. History—and the time line—ends at the coming of God's kingdom. When we talk about the Second Coming and the General Resurrection in the Creed, we are not proclaiming a historical moment but rather the *direction* and *purpose* toward which all history moves, God's purpose. The resurrected life is our participation in this goal.

The Roman Catholic Pierre Benoit has written, ". . . if according to the traditional faith we must believe that our bodies will rise at the end of the old world in which we are still immersed, at the same time we must acknowledge that we have no idea at all of what this end of our times corresponds with in the new and already present world in which the risen Christ lives. And since, in addition, we know that we are already united here below in the Holy Spirit with the body of the risen Christ, we are able to believe that directly after death we shall find in this uninterrupted union the source and means of our essential blessedness."[3]

There is no man, no matter how firm his commitment, who at the moment of death is perfectly ready for God's kingdom. Every man presents himself as he is. What is important is his responsiveness to God as the God of truth is known to him, his openness to the power and love of Jesus Christ as declared to him. God in Christ can continue to perfect him after death as surely as he does before. Thus our union with Christ, begun at our Baptism and realized to some degree in our earthly life, continues through death and ultimately into resurrected life with him.

[3]"Resurrection: At the End of Time or Immediately after Death?" in *Immortality and Resurrection*, edited by Pierre Benoit and Roland Murphy. New York: The Seabury Press (Concilium series), 1970, p. 114.

9

EUCHARISTIC LIVING/DYING

The Consecration: Part B

"And I know that his commandment [of loving fellowship] *is eternal life."*

John 12:50

For some strange reason, the more sophisticated we become in our technology, the more primitive we tend to remain in our appreciation of God's wonderful universe. We were amused, not surprised, when the first Russian cosmonaut with a bit of self-satisfaction solemnly (though childishly) announced upon his return that he had not seen God in his orbital trip. We all still tend to speak—and think—of "heaven" as being "up" and of "hell" as being "down." So long as we are speaking qualitatively, we are accurate. But when we try to locate heaven, even in our thoughts, we are in trouble. What really do we mean by "up"? Since we are at all times related to some spot on this spheroid we call earth, would it not be at least more accurate to speak of "out" (meaning away from the earth) and "in" (meaning toward its center)? Is "heaven" then "out" and hell "in"?

Biblical thought is set within a very limited cosmology. The universe is a three-storied affair with heaven above the earth and hell below. There are waters above the firmament (the sky), and there are waters below the earth. God's realm is above. Thus he sends "down" both his Son and his Spirit. But Copernicus changed that way of thinking for all time, and it is not really essential to understanding Biblical truth. Indeed, such a primitive cosmology is a real handicap to understanding the message of the Gospel for us today. The truth of God is not wedded to any particular way of looking at the world about us. There is the need for continuing reinterpretation of the Good News for us in terms we can appreciate. It was equally important when the New Testament was being written that it be stated in a manner compatible with the understanding the people of that day had of their world.

We have already said that it is not of the essence of Christian belief to hold that at death the soul is freed from a worn out or destroyed physical body and flies to a spiritual state to join other spirits, forever leaving behind this temporary sphere we call the world. Indeed, this is not consistent with the body/soul unity the Bible insists every person truly is. Certainly we do not believe that Jesus upon his death ceased to have any further relationship with this world. On the contrary, we firmly believe that because of his death his presence is no longer limited by a physical body to a particular spot in Palestine. We believe that he is truly *everywhere,* on this earth and in the universe. No matter to what constellation future astronauts may roam, Jesus Christ is ever present with them, around them, in them—and he is at their destination before them. Jesus is even now and always in contact with all men —whether they realize it or not. The Gospel proclaims it joyfully, "Lo, I am with you always . . ." (Matthew 28:20).

If Christ is the "author and finisher" of our faith, he has led where we can follow. If our life now and beyond death is dependent upon our relationship with Christ, we must be with him "where he is." Where he is, is right here as well as out there. Christ is not divorced from matter. He is just no longer *dependent* upon a material body to express his reality. Thus "the soul's freeing from the body in death does not just mean a withdrawal from matter. Rather, it signifies the entering into a closer proximity with matter, into a relation with the world extended to cosmic proportions."[1]

The physical body each of us now possesses is both the means for expressing our real personhood and a hindrance to the full expression of that personhood. Each of us is ensheathed in a

[1]Boros, *op. cit.,* p. 148.

seamless skin, a dermal envelope that holds together our instrument of expression in this physical world. This enfleshed body enables us to
enter into relationships with others, which foster
and nourish our growth—and theirs—into the
persons that we and they now are. But at the
same time the body and its enveloping sheath
makes demands of its own upon us and leads us
at times to function in ways that abuse and destroy our relationships with others. We, in turn,
are diminished. Furthermore, even in our closest
encounter with another human being, even in
the most intimate of human relationships, our
dermal envelope completely contains us as a
glove does a hand. We can move about, approach
others, love them; but we can never pierce that
thin sheath which absolutely prevents the ultimate intimacy and union for which we yearn.

Christ shared the same kind of body in his
earthly life. The consecration of his death rests
in the fact that in his death, in his freedom from
the old body and his taking up of a new body, he
came into the unity that is at the root of God's
world. Now the agent of creation was "poured
out" in his redemptive death over that creation
which he not only began but now redeems. "We
know that the whole creation has been groaning
in travail together until now . . ." (Romans 8:22).
Upon his death, the soul/body of Christ entered
into a new and intimate relationship with all that
is and ever has been and ever will be. Is it not

proper to think of Christ not as "a-cosmic," removed from all matter, but rather as
"*all*-cosmic," permeating everything? Is this not
really more consistent with scriptural insistence
upon the universal presence of Christ? If we can
think of God at the very least as the foundation
of all being, undergirding and holding everything
together, from the tiniest parts of the atom to the
most distant constellations, we can also think of
Christ through his death as relating intimately to
all things so that the world and the whole universe have become the "bodily instrument of
Christ's humanity . . . ,"[2] giving a new holiness
and a new significance to that very world of
which we are now a part.

We can then see that what the Creed calls
Christ's "descent into hell" is a far more significant fact than going down into the bowels of
the earth to preach to men who had died before
his coming, or merely lingering in a suspended
state of disembodied spirit awaiting resurrection.
The word "hell" itself troubles us because we
invariably confuse two New Testament concepts
by often translating two very different words with
the same word, "hell." In the New Testament,
there is a distinction between "hades," the abode
of the departed, and "Gehenna," the place of tor-
ture of the damned. The modern translations of
the New Testament are careful to differentiate;

[2]*Ibid.*, p. 149.

but the confusion in our minds still lingers from
the Authorized Version's translation of both
words as "hell." *The Book of Common Prayer*
notes in its rubric before the Apostles' Creed that
"any Churches may, instead of the words, He descended into hell, use the words, He went into
the place of departed spirits, which are considered as words of the same meaning in the
Creed" (p. 15). Never have I worshipped at a service at which such a substitution was made. The
new translation of the Apostles' Creed proposed
by the International Conference on English
Texts suggests "He descended to the dead." Yet
even in this no doubt accurate translation of
words, we are still troubled by the word "descended," which implies a direction rather than a
purpose.

At his death Christ, the author of creation,
infused all creation with his redemptive love. His
death was not for man alone, but for all that he
had made. The death of Christ was not an extin-
guishing of the "light that shines in the dark"
but rather a carrying forth of that light of God's
life and love into all the vast recesses of creation.
At last God stood fully revealed, uncovered.
Man—and the world—could now look upon God
and live!

Christ's "descent," then, is his permeation of
all creation with his life and love. Even now all
that is can convey the ever-present light of Christ
to the eye that will see. Christ is united with all

his creation, and through his creation he is continuing even now his work of reconciliation.

Consecration is the point at which God takes the offering and transforms it. So in the consecration of his death, God takes the life of Christ and unites him with all that is, with the world and with us. Thus, in Christ, death becomes not the moment of absolute separation, but the beginning of a wondrous unity. We do not have to pinpoint "paradise" or "purgatory" or the "intermediate state." Our beloved dead are "in Christ" and Christ is in all things and everywhere. Loving fellowship cannot be destroyed by physical separation, not even the separation of death. In Christ we are united with all others who are in him. We do not have to wait until we die to be united with those whom we love who die in Christ. We are united now, in that kind of unpossessive union that is love at its finest. The consecration of life is in its becoming whole and perfect. The one essential quality of that wholeness is unity with all that is God's.

10

EUCHARISTIC LIVING/DYING

The Communion

*Jesus took bread, and blessed, and broke it, and
gave it to the disciples and said, "Take, eat;
this is my body." And he took a cup, and when
he had given thanks he gave it to them, saying,
"Drink of it, all of you; for this is my blood ..."*

Matthew 26 : 26f

Teilhard de Chardin, the late geologist and paleontologist as well as Roman Catholic priest, had a lifelong concern to bring science and Christianity together in a new way, because he was convinced that the data of both are valid and necessary for modern man. "This he tried to do primarily because he believed that Christ, as God incarnate, revealed in himself not only the mystery of God but also the meaning of man, and therefore the ultimate meaning of that evolutionary process of which God is the cause and man the culmination. . . . For many a good Christian, he once noted, the universe is transparent; it stands between himself and God but he does not see it at all. For the unbeliever, on the other

92

hand, the universe is opaque and he can see nothing else."[1] Each of these views, Teilhard says, is equally inaccurate. As both a theologian and a scientist he was convinced that we can meet Christ everywhere because throughout the whole universe an essential "Christ dimension" can be seen by the discerning eye.

The death of Jesus did not cut him off from the world of matter. Indeed, since he was no longer enfleshed in one body in one place and time, by his descent into the very heart of all being with God himself, he is now intimately related with all that is. He is a part of all being, ever seeking to bring about God's intended unity of the universe.

Christ is everywhere, undergirding all that is. There is no thing, no person, no event in which Christ cannot be seen and heard and felt—experienced by the sensitive Christian soul.

> " ' . . . I was hungry and you gave me food,
> I was thirsty and you gave me drink,
> I was a stranger and you welcomed me,
> I was naked and you clothed me,
> I was sick and you visited me,
> I was in prison and you came to me . . . .
> Truly, I say to you, as you did it to one
> of the least of these my brethren,
> you did it to me.' "

Matthew 25:35, 36, 40

[1] As interpreted by Christopher F. Mooney, S.J., "A Fresh Look at Man," *Saturday Review*, February 26, 1966, p. 21.

Christ's "descent," his intimate involvement in
all that is, helps us see how indeed our actions
as they affect any part of God's creation—even
ourselves—are done to Christ himself. This is
not mere poetry. This is reality.

Yet such discernment requires the quality of
faith, just as the miracle of healing in the woman
at Capernaum required the quality of faith. In
the press of the crowd Jesus was jostled and
pushed by many. But one woman in need and
faith touched the hem of his garment deliberately—and she was cured. Though many handled
him physically at that time, only one really
touched him. She touched him both physically and spiritually. She touched with all the
reaching out she could muster. In that touch he
reached in with his healing power. Herein is
communion: the reaching out and the reaching
in. Christ is everywhere, in everything, in
everyone, and so especially in the consecrated
bread and wine through which he has promised
to make himself real to us. We reach out to him
in faith and he reaches in to us in love. This is
communion—not a one-way receiving of grace,
but a two-way offering and receiving of selves.
As we know him in this special moment before
his altar, so we begin to know him in all things,
in all persons, in all places, in all times.

The barriers Christ transcends are not
merely temporal and spatial. I believe commu-

nion goes much deeper and can become very personal. Because Christ offers all persons, living and departed, this special communion with him, so in him we have the possibility of communion with our beloved dead. If in his death Christ has become not "a-cosmic," cut off from the universe, but "all-cosmic," permeating all matter and reality, surely those who die in Christ are not removed from the world to a never-never land of the spirit. On the contrary, in Christ they are more closely related to the whole of the world in a new and ever-enlarging way. In our communion with Christ, then, there is also the possibility for communion with everyone who is in him. "For I am sure that neither death, nor life, nor angels, nor principalities, nor things present, nor things to come, nor powers, nor height, nor depth, nor anything else in all creation, will be able to separate us from the love of God in Christ Jesus our Lord" (Romans 8:38f). Not only do these "things" not necessarily separate us; indeed in Christ these "things" are able to bind us together with him and with one another. "The communion of the saints" that we profess in the creeds is the union of believers everywhere, whether this side of the grave or the other, guaranteed by the love of Jesus Christ.

A Belgian father relates that during his early bereavement for his son killed in World War II, he looked up one evening from his paper to see his wife smiling over her sewing. " 'How can you

possibly be happy—now?' he demanded. 'Because
I believe that Pieter also is happy, and that he
wants us to be happy, because I am with him all
the time and bring him into everything we think
or do in his old home. Happiness, as I understand it, is not the absence of suffering.' "[2]

This is not just a memory that is held on to
and that fades away or perishes when those who
remember die. This communion with the dead
can be very real. But "communion of the saints,"
whether departed saints or living, must not be
confused in any way with the varied occult efforts so popular today to "communicate" with
the dead, which seem more as attempts to *use*
the dead for personal satisfaction than to enter
into communion with them. The communion
Christians can experience with their departed
friends in the faith is an *internal* rather than ex-
ternal reality, similar to that warmth of trans-
cending love we experience at times when sepa-
rated geographically from those with whom we
are bound in love. It is not verbal; it cannot be
conjured up at our whim or through our effort. It
is a "glow" that most often comes unexpectedly.
We are surprised, delighted, enriched,
strengthened. My experience is that one of the
most fruitful times for such "communions" is
while worshiping at Holy Communion. And why
shouldn't it be, for at such a time we are likely to

be "in tune" with our Lord and it is solely through him that such personal communions can and do take place. Is it not also reasonable, then, that the dead in Christ can, through him, have communion among themselves?

Cammaerts affirms his own growing awareness and experience. "Death is no insuperable barrier, but it is a barrier which cannot be forced by man. Pieter is with me today, not because I remember him or because his ghost chooses to visit me, but because we are bound together by the love we share. His presence is not a mirage, but a real thing, most vivid and often unexpected. He appears to me as he was because, no doubt, I should not be able to recognize him if he appeared otherwise. I can only pray that the gift of death will open my eyes to his true personality, which I only comprehended imperfectly a year ago and which I may be allowed to comprehend hereafter."[3]

"The gift of death." What a tremendous insight!

"This is my body...this is my blood...." What a tremendous act of love!

Death in Christ is not the closing of a door but the opening up of possibilities for new and deeper and freer relationships. A new life, a new being lies before us—new life and new being with which we can be in communion even now.

[3]*Ibid.,* p. 70.

Far from destroying communion with those whom we love in Christ, death can open up for us the deepest kind of communion, the kind that gives without demanding, the kind of *agape* love we know to be of the nature of God, the foretaste of heaven itself.

11

EUCHARISTIC LIVING/DYING

The Thanksgiving

Almighty and everlasting God, we most heartily thank thee . . . that we are very members incorporate in the mystical body of thy Son, which is the blessed company of all faithful people; and are also heirs through hope of thy everlasting kingdom. . . .

The Book of Common Prayer, p. 83.

Death and grief are twin companions. We experience grief as we struggle to determine who we are and realize that a person who gives us meaning is leaving us forever by death. We depend upon our relationships with others to give us a sense of identity. So when a supportive person is no longer available, we are changed; we must rediscover ourselves, rebuild our identity. The process of recovery from grief depends greatly upon a successful reconstruction of our life.

The dying man, the person who knows he is dying, has a similar struggle, for he sees not one but *all* of his relationships crumbling—he faces the great loneliness that this apparently complete separation foretells. Even a very sick person who, in the face of relentless pain, yearns for the release that only death can bring still struggles at the same time with this lonely uncertainty.

Our culture—which includes our religious heritage—confronts us with death as the destruction of all that a man has achieved in life as well as with the removal of his spiritual essence, his personality, his soul, to some remote corner of reality far from all that is familiar and dear. Whether this be called "Abraham's bosom" or "paradise" or "purgatory" or simply "eternal rest," the condition is hardly one that is inviting, much less enticing. Indeed, it strikes a fearful note in the hearts of most people.

The death of Christ shows us that this is not the complete picture of death, for, through Easter eyes, we see in his dying upon the cross not the negation and destruction of his manhood, but the affirmation of his real being. Furthermore, his death did not remove the reality of his presence to some remote corner of the universe, but through his death his presence has become universal, closer, more intimate than when he was physically present.

So the first followers of Jesus turned quickly from sadness to joy. The bitterness of the cross gave way to glory and death took on a new dimension. How else can one explain that marvelous transformation of the men who on Good Friday fled and hid, only to go forth courageously in due time to offer their own lives in their Lord's service? There *is* a glory to death—the glory of Christ's death, the glory of our own death in Christ, the glory of the deaths of those we love in him. The early Christians saw the glory and the possibilities of death and so they glorified the martyrs, those who died with an affirmation of themselves for God and for his Christ.

St. John Chrysostom wrote of the glory of death to a bereaved friend of the fourth century. "Thou hast not lost thy son but bestowed him henceforth in Eternity.... That is not thy child that is lying there. He has flown away and sprung aloft into boundless height. When, then, thou seest the eyes closed, the lips locked together, the body motionless, oh, be not these thy thoughts:

'These lips no longer speak,
these eyes no longer see,
these feet no longer walk, but are all on their way to
corruption.'

Oh, say not so; but say the reverse:

'These lips shall speak better,
these eyes shall see greater things,
these feet shall mount upon the clouds,

>   and this body . . . shall put on immortality,
>   and I shall receive my son back more glorious.' "[1]

So St. Paul could exclaim, "Far be it from me to glory except in the cross of our Lord Jesus Christ . . ." (Galatians 6:14).

If death has no meaning, life has no real destiny. It is futile. "Was it for this the clay grew tall?" Yes, we must affirm; yes, it was for this —for death. But death is not the end of life; this, too, we must affirm. Death is not even the gateway to life everlasting through which every man must pass. Death is the *event* in the continuing process of life in which at last a man is completely free to affirm God and his Christ forever. Death is the event that brings our personal humanity to a focus, to fulfillment. Death is the event through our fellowship with Christ that brings our personal life into vital contact with the entire universe and with the very foundation stone of the universe—God himself. Death is the event which, instead of destroying relationships, opens them up to new dimensions, new expressions. Death does not separate—rather in Christ death unites us in the perfect union God intends. Death in fellowship with Christ is the event that frees and empowers us to be what we really yearn to be.

The curious thing is that persistent thought about death inevitably leads to consideration of

[1] Quoted by Cammaerts, *op. cit.*, pp. 117f.

life, life in two directions: the resurrection life, and that life here and now which is invariably shaped by our convictions about death and resurrection. The main qualification the first Christian community had for a replacement for Iscariot was one able to witness to the Resurrection of Jesus. Easter is the heart of the Good News—not just because it promises a future, but also because it gives the present moment both direction and hope. If death in Christ is the event that permits a person the freedom finally to affirm his reality and being, then each small affirmation now on the way of life is a steppingstone to that final leap. If death does not forever separate us from those we love, but rather opens a new dimension to our relationship with them, then each relationship we develop now—or deny now—has eternal implications for us.

A view of the glory of death gives us hope and encouragement to seek the fullness of life now. The clay grows tall that it may cease to be mere clay and become progressively a vital part of God's eternal reality, preserving all the while its uniqueness as a child of God. Death need not be our enemy, but—in Christ—the event that brings freedom and unity and fulfillment, indeed, the peace that passes our present understanding. "Thanks be to God, who gives us the victory through our Lord Jesus Christ" (1 Corinthians 15:57).

Praise be, my Lord, through our Sister Bodily
Death
From whom no man living can escape.

SELECTED
BIBLIOGRAPHY

Books and Articles

Adams, James R., *The Sting of Death.* New York: The Seabury Press, 1971. Leader's guide for a study course on death and bereavement.

Barthel, Joan, " 'I Promise You, It Will Be All Right'—The Dilemma of a Friend's Dying." *Life,* Vol. 72, No. 10, March 17, 1972.

Becker, Ernest, *The Denial of Death.* New York: The Free Press, 1973.

Benoit, Pierre and Roland Murphy, editors, *Immortality and Resurrection.* New York: The Seabury Press, 1970.

Boros, Ladislaus, *The Mystery of Death.* New York: The Seabury Press, 1965.

Cammaerts, Emil, *Upon This Rock.* New York: Harper and Bros., 1943.

Doyle, Nancy, "The Dying Person and the Family." New York: Public Affairs Pamphlet No. 485, 1972.

Emrich, Richard S., *Death and Hope.* Cincinnati: The Forward Movement, n.d., a pamphlet.

Feifel, Herman, editor, *The Meaning of Death.* New York: McGraw-Hill Book Company, Inc., 1959.

Forsyth, P. T., *The Cruciality of the Cross*. London: Independent Press, Ltd., 1948.

Gibson, Paul, "The Agony of Dying." *Frontier*, Vol. 4, No. 3, Winter 1960.

Green, Betty R. and Donald P. Irish, editors, *Death Education: Preparation for Living*. Cambridge, Mass.: Schenkman Publishing Co., 1971.

Hayes, John D., "What Is Death?" *Listening*, Vol. 2, No. 1, Winter 1967.

Jorjorian, Armen D., "Ministry at the Point of Death." *St. Luke's Journal*, Vol. XIV, No. 2, March 1971. Sewanee, Tenn.: The University of the South, 1971.

Krant, Melvin J., "The Organized Care of the Dying." *Hospital Practice*, Vol. 7, No. 1, January 1972.

Kübler-Ross, Elisabeth, *On Death and Dying*. New York: The Macmillan Co., 1970. Now available in paperback.

Lackmann, Max, "Death and Resurrection." *Listening*, Vol. 3, No. 1, Winter 1968.

Lifton, Robert Jay and Eric Olson, *Living and Dying*. New York: Praeger Publishers, 1974.

May, Rollo, *Love and Will*. New York: W.W. Norton & Co., 1969.

Mitford, Jessica, *The American Way of Death*. New York: Simon and Schuster, 1963. Published in paperback in 1969 by Fawcett-World.

Moltmann, Jürgen, "Eternity." *Listening*, Vol. 3, No. 2, Spring 1968.

Mooney, Christopher F., "A Fresh Look at Man." *Saturday Review*, February 26, 1966.

Owen, Wilfred, *Collected Poems,* edited with an Introduction and Notes by C. Day Lewis and with a Memoir by Edmund Blunden. Norfolk, Conn.: New Directions, 1964.

Penick, Edwin Anderson, "Life After Death." Cincinnati: Forward Movement Publications, 1970, a pamphlet.

Rahner, Karl, *On the Theology of Death,* No. 2 in *Quaestiones Disputatae.* New York: The Seabury Press, 1962.

Ramsey, Michael, *Christ Crucified for the World.* New York: Morehouse-Barlow Co., Inc., 1964.

————, *The Resurrection of Christ.* Glasgow: William Collins Sons & Co., Ltd., 1961.

Reed, Elizabeth L., *Helping Children with the Mystery of Death.* Nashville: Abingdon Press, 1970.

Saunders, Cicely, "And From Sudden Death . . ." *Frontier,* Vol. 4, Winter 1961.

Services for Trial Use. New York: The Church Hymnal Corporation, 1971.

Sheppard, Gordon, *The Man Who Gave Himself Away,* illustrated by Jacques Rozier. New York: Harlin Quist, Inc. (Franklin Watts, Inc.), 1971.

Shinn, Roger Lincoln, *Life, Death, and Destiny.* Philadelphia: The Westminster Press, 1957. In the *Layman's Theological Library* series, Robert McAfee Brown, general editor.

Stephens, Simon, *Death Comes Home.* New York: Morehouse-Barlow Co., 1973.

Stringfellow, William, *Instead of Death.* New York: The Seabury Press, 1963.

Thielicke, Helmut, *Death and Life,* together with a "Letter to a Soldier about Death." Philadelphia: Fortress Press, 1970.

Weatherhead, Leslie D., *The Will of God.* Nashville: Abingdon Press, 1944.

Cassettes

Kübler-Ross, Elisabeth, "Ministering to the Terminally Ill," 29½ minutes, Vol. 3, No. 3, 1972. Thesis Theological Cassettes. P. O. Box 11724, Pittsburgh, Pa. 15228.

Shneidman, Edwin S., "Death, The Enemy." Del Mar, Calif.: Psychology Today, 1973.

Thielicke, Helmut, "Death and Eternal Life," two cassettes and response guide, 1972. Creative Resources, Box 1790, Waco, Texas 76703.

Films

To Die Today, featuring Dr. Elisabeth Kübler-Ross, 16mm film from CBC. Available through Jeanine Locke, Thursday Night Producer, CBC, 135 Maitland Street, Toronto, Canada.

Until I Die, featuring Dr. Elisabeth Kübler-Ross, 16mm film produced by WTTW, Channel 11, Chicago. Distributed through Video Nursing, Inc., 2834 Central Street, Evanston Ill. 60201. Attention: Joan Joyce.

Throughout the United States and Canada there are more than a hundred local memorial societies dedicated to simplicity, dignity, and economy in funeral arrangements. While these are not necessarily Christian organizations as such, they are often initiated by church or ministerial associations and can be helpful in guiding those who wish to plan for their funerals with an emphasis upon the continuation of life. For more information, write:

Continental Association
1828 L Street, N.W.
Washington , D.C. 20036

Memorial Society Association of Canada
5326 Ada Boulevard
Edmonton, Alberta T5W 4N T , Canada

Available through both associations is *A Manual of Simple Burial* by Ernest Morgan, a 64-page booklet providing information on making simple funeral arrangements and directories of local memorial societies. Also available is "Putting My House In Order," a convenient two-page form for recording a multitude of information needed at the time of death.

Helpful information on "How the Dead Can Help the Living" is included in *A Manual of Simple Burial* with particular attention to the donation of one's body or specific organs or tissues. The Uniform Donor Card is a legal document in most states and provinces. Copies are often available locally. It is designed to be carried in a wallet.

UNIFORM DONOR CARD

OF_____
Print or type name of donor

In the hope that I may help others, I hereby make this anatomical gift, if medically acceptable, to take effect upon my death. The words and marks below indicate my desires.

I give: (a) _____ any needed organs or parts
        (b) _____ only the following organs or parts

_____
Specify the organ(s) or part(s)

for the purposes of transplantation, therapy, medical research or education;

        (c) _____ my body for anatomical study if needed.

Limitations or
special wishes, if any :_____

Signed by the donor and the following two witnesses in the presence of each other:

_____   _____
Signature of Donor   Date of Birth of Donor

_____   _____
Date Signed   City & State

_____   _____
Witness   Witness

This is a legal document under the Uniform Anatomical Gift Act or similar laws.

For further information consult your local memorial society or
Continental Association of Funeral & Memorial Societies
1828 L Street N.W., Washington, D.C. 20036